DRAVIDIAN ARCHITECTURE

DRAVIDIAN ARCHITECTURE

G. JOUVEAU-DUBREUIL

EDITED WITH PREFACE AND NOTES
S. KRISHNASWAMI AIYANGAR

GYAN

Published by

Gyan Publishing House
5, Ansari Road
Daryaganj, New Delhi-110002
Phone: 011-47034999, 9811692060
E-mail: books@gyanbooks.com

Distribution Network
gyanbooks.com
India, USA, Canada, UK, Australia, France

ISBN : 978-81-212-4512-8 (HB)
First Published, 1917

2nd Impression 2020

Printed at: Gyan Press, Delhi.

Dravindian Architecture
Author: G. Jouveau-Dubreuil

DRAVIDIAN ARCHITECTURE

BY

G. JOUVEAU-DUBREUIL

Professor, the College, Pondichery.
Doctor of the University of Paris

Edited with Preface and Notes

BY

S. KRISHNASWAMI AIYANGAR

M.A., M.R.A.S., F.R. HIST. S.

Professor of Indian History and Archaeology,
University of Madras,

Fellow of the University of Madras
Fellow of the Mysore University

MADRAS

PRINTED AT THE S.P.C.K. PRESS, VEPERY

1917

EDITOR'S PREFACE

THE institution of a chair of Indian History and Archæology at the University of Madras gives evidence of the rising interest in these subjects not only at the University but also among the cultured public. That this interest should be so directed as to make it fruitful, few will deny. It is with a view to stimulate interest in one of the subjects comprised in the term Archæology, and direct that interest into fruitful fields of work that this little handbook has been rendered into English and published in the present form. I made the acquaintance of the talented author of the French work the *Archæology and Iconography of South India* (published by Paul-Geuthner of Paris in the *Annales Musée Guimet*), through a review of the work in the *Journal of the Royal Asiatic Society* by Mr. R. Sewell. In the course of a growing acquaintance his suggestion that a handbook, such as the one here offered to the public would be useful, struck me as a very good one, and I readily took upon myself the responsibility of bringing out this English version of his French work, which is rather of the nature of an introduction to the subject of his larger work than an abridgment of it. He has since brought out in English, Part I of his *Pallava Antiquities* which gives ample evidence of what systematic work in subjects like this can achieve. This introduction is intended to enable such systematic work being undertaken with success by those to whom a regular course of training is impossible.

The French text of the author was done into English for me by my friend Mr. K. Amrita Rau, M.A., Reader in Dravidian Philology, University of Madras, to whom it gives me the greatest pleasure to acknowledge my obligations. The translation had the benefit of Professor G. Jouveau-Dubreuil's own revision, and has his approval in the form in which it appears.

In case this should find welcome among those interested in these unremunerative, though far from unpleasing, studies,

I shall be happy to go further forward and provide introductory manuals in other allied subjects, such as Epigraphy, Numismatics, etc., with the assistance of specialists in these various branches. I take this occasion to acknowledge my deep debt of obligation to Professor Jouveau-Dubreuil for his disinterested labours for this little book, and place the book before the learned public in the hope that both he and his. editor, will have the great satisfaction of an appreciative reception which is the highest reward which labourers in such fields have at all a right to expect. It is hoped that University students will take kindly to this subject, so that when they pass out of the University into the various walks of life, they may find in this, the opening for an enjoyable hobby, each according to his or her opportunities.

'Śrīvāsam', S. KRISHNASWAMI AIYANGAR.
Mylapore, Madras, S,
October 22, 1916.

CHAPTER I

GENERAL OBSERVATION

WE propose to study here the architecture of that part of Southern India which extends along the Coromandel Coast from Lake Pulicat to Cape Comorin. This architecture is distinguished very clearly from that of the neighbouring countries, and as it concerns entirely and exclusively the country occupied by the Tamils, that is the people who speak Tamil, we shall give it the name 'Dravidian Architecture' since the two words 'Tamil' and 'Dravidian' are in reality one and the same word, having absolutely the same etymology. We shall study, however, more especially a very limited part of the Tamil country which includes the three districts of Chingleput, North Arcot and South Arcot. It is possible to make a precise study only by closely limiting the field of that study.

Religious edifices are extremely numerous in the South of India. They are found everywhere, in big towns, in villages, in the forest; almost all these monuments are covered with inscriptions, and before writing the history of their architecture, it is necessary to translate these inscriptions and to study the form of the character, because one can often thus discover the age, if not of the monument itself, at least of the inscription.

The patient efforts of historians and epigraphists have succeeded in establishing some facts from amongst a mass of uncertainties and contradictions.

Special works: *South Indian Inscriptions. Epigraphia Indica, Indian Antiquary, Government Orders on Annual Reports on Epigraphy* (Southern Circle), these contain innumerable documents upon the subject.

These historical works have served, on the one hand, to make the numbering of a great part of the more important monuments possible; on the other hand, to determine the age of some of them.

The art itself has been very much neglected. And yet if any of the monuments have been abundantly described and photographed, they are the pagodas of Southern India. The temples of Tanjore, Trichinopoly, Madura, form part of a classical tour, and tourists who go to India never fail to visit them before going to see Benares and the Taj. There exists besides a great number of accounts of travels in which the pagodas are described, and illustrated often by very beautiful pictures.

The descriptions and the photographs are, it is true, very precious materials for the study of that art; they are documents indispensable to archæologists who have not been in the country and who cannot study the objects themselves; but that does not constitute a study; there is a difference between describing and studying. Most of the authors who have treated Dravidian art do not seem to have sufficiently made that distinction. A book on architecture should not resemble a tourist's guide. It is necessary not only to make one see things, but to make one comprehend them, to evolve general ideas and to discover principles. It is, therefore, necessary to compare the monuments everywhere, to give them a systematic classification and to set forth the laws according to which they have been constructed. It is a matter of great importance to describe the anatomy and the palæontology of the edifices.

We now propose not to recommence, as it has been done a thousand times, the particular description of some edifices considered individually. We shall try to make the science of monuments, by an attempt to discover general laws by the comparative study of the *motifs* of ornamentation.

Works of art, indeed, are not made entirely at random from inspiration; there are almost always discoverable some methods, principles and invariable canonical rules. Whatever may be the originality of a work of art, it is rarely an isolated work; it is connected with contemporary works; it is explained by anterior works. The author belongs to a school, the work belongs to a style.

There is nobody who cannot distinguish the Greek style from the Gothic. Further, in the same Greek style, there are the Doric, Ionian, and Corinthian; and in the Gothic style, one distinguishes primary, secondary and tertiary styles.

If we consider from this point of view the architecture of the South of India, we can prove that here also exist very definite styles. It is necessary then to distinguish them one from the other and to determine exactly the character of each of them.

But, first of all, let us examine a very important fact which will considerably simplify the question. By comparing the style of monuments with the palæographic indications given by the inscriptions engraved upon the monuments, we find that every style corresponds to a chronological epoch.

Every edifice can perhaps be characterized by its ornamentation; but there exist others which have the same ornamentation; we can then prove that these other monuments date from the same epoch. Finally, if we examine the edifices which have a different style, we can prove that they are also of different epochs. Having then observed that monuments of one style are of the same age, we also come to the conclusion reciprocally that to every epoch there is, in the Dravidian country, only a single style. This is what we shall characterize as the 'Principle of the Synchronism of Dravidian Styles.'

Thus then modern monuments do not resemble ancient monuments; they are not of the same style. How are these changes produced; at what epoch and for what reason have they stopped constructing in a particular manner, and why again have they constructed in a different manner?

The first hypothesis which presents itself to the mind to explain these modifications is foreign influence.

But in investigating the origin of styles, we have been led to discover a fact which we were very far from expecting, which nothing could make us guess, and which renders the study of Dravidian art extremely interesting.[1] That is that there has never been foreign influence. It is possible to find out in the ancient Dravidian monuments the origin of all the *motifs* of ornamentation which characterize the modern styles, and on the whole, Dravidian art has changed of itself. We shall ex-

[1] Recent researches have led to the same conclusion in respect of Egyptian architecture as well. (*Vide* p. 38 note, and the remarks of Lepsius translated in Appendix A of *Egyptian Architecture* by Edward Bell, Messrs. Bell & Sons London.).—*S. K.*

press this idea by saying that it has changed by 'the path of natural evolution.'

An analogous fact is produced by the French architecture of the Middle Ages. We know that the first idea was to explain origin its by the influence of barbarians, and we have given to French architecture the name Gothic. We see it written later on that the art appeared in consequençe of the Saracenic conquests, or rather that the *Ogival* art had been imported into France on the return of the Crusaders from the country of the Mussalmans. It is only by the systematic study of the history of religious edifices of the Middle Ages that one arrives at the conclusion that the Gothic art is purely French, that it was born, not upon the banks of the Rhine or upon the shores of the Mediterranean, but in the 'Ile de France,' and that it is the 'Romanesque Architecture' which, gradually by 'the path of natural evolution' has changed into Gothic.

It is necessary, in reality, to distinguish between an 'Evolution' and a 'Revolution'.

If, on account of a conquest, an invasion, a fashion, or other causes, the workmen of a country change at a certain epoch, their methods of work and begin to employ *motifs* of ornamentation entirely different, for a long time, because they are inspired by *motifs* belonging to the style of another country or another age, there is a revolution in architecture.

In order that there may be an evolution, it is necessary that the change of *motifs* of ornamentation should be made gradually and by the very force of things. The workmen are not inspired by foreign *motifs*, but by the continual employment of their methods; they are by themselves led to modify their technique.

Thus, it is by the path of natural evolution that the 'Romanesque Architecture' has been transformed into the Gothic. It is also by evolution that the Gothic has been transformed gradually until it became the Flamboyant; but it is not by evolution, but by a sort of revolution, that, being inspired by Greek and Roman architectures, the French workmen abandoned almost completely the *motifs* which their ancestors had created and constructed the monuments which characterize the renaissance.

In France this evolution was very rapid. In the South of India, on account of the traditional conservatism of the Hindus this evolution was very slow, and it is during fourteen centuries that the architectural transformations were produced.

The Dravidian art presents to us a very interesting and very rare picture of an architecture which remained isolated for more than thirteen centuries, which borrowed nothing from foreign arts, but which varied continually by the path of natural evolution, in such a way that one could follow its modifications from one century to another.

On the whole, in the South of India, every epoch has been marked by a definite style, which is explained by the style of the preceding epoch and which serves to explain the style of the following epoch; and the morphology of the Dravidian monuments teaches us that the forms of architecture have been transformed slowly, just as the prehistoric anthropology shows us that the human skull has passed through all the intermediary stages between the ape-like form and the actual human form. There is the same difference between the style of the *Rathas* of the 'Seven-Pagodas' (Māmallapuram) and the style of the temple at Tiruppāpuliyūr (Cuddalore, New Town), as between the skull of a man of the race of Cromagnon and the skull of a modern man.

The existence of a very definite architectural style in the Tamil country and the evolution of the style could be explained easily.

From ancient times up to our days, the pagodas have been constructed by workmen who formed an organized corporation.

The master-masons constructed always according to the methods of their time with the *motifs* which their ancestors had transmitted to them. On account of the very special geographical position of Southern India, the workmen of the Tamil country were not always in direct communication[1] with

[1] There are references in the ancient classics of Tamil, that jewellers from Maghada, masons from Mārāṭṭa, blacksmiths from Avanti (Mālva) and carpentors from Yavana, co-operated in the construction of Kaveripaṭṭinam at the mouth of the Kaveri (*Maṇimēkhalai*, Canto XIX : ll. 107-110). There is a similar instance of co-operation among master craftsmen elsewhere; the Yavana carpenter, Mālva blacksmith, the Maghada jeweller, goldsmith from somewhere else, the picture writers of Kosala and the painters of Vatsa, (Kōsambi).—*S.K.*

the workmen of other countries, and had never any occasion to be inspired by foreign styles.

During several generations of workmen the manner of work of the sculptor remained almost invariable. But yet in the course of centuries the sculptural renderings were transformed insensibly.

We shall not attempt to discover the causes of these modifications. This phenomenon is not particular to architecture: it is general. The form of characters of the alphabet which were used in writing Tamil have been transformed in the course of centuries. The language has been transformed also, in the same manner as usages and manners have been gradually transformed. Religion itself has also been modified, and in our days the rites and dogmas are not absolutely the same as those during the epoch of the Pallavas; it is often very easy to distinguish a modern image from another more ancient.

It is not then only by the architectural style that one recognizes the age of a monument, but also by iconography; that, is to say the study of the images which adorn the temple; but it is above all by the form of the characters of the alphabet of the inscriptions which are often engraved on the monument that this distinction can be made with safety if not with absolute certainty. We shall, however, confine ourselves here to the study of architectural forms according to the epochs and in estimating the age of the monument we shall rely upon the information furnished by epigraphy and palæography.

We shall choose them in the very restricted part of the Tamil country which we have selected (districts of Chingleput, North Arcot, South Arcot) a certain number of monuments the age of which has been well determined with the aid of inscriptions which are engraved on them, so as to have at least one specimen of architecture of each epoch.

While comparing the monuments (one monument with another) we shall be able to verify the exactness of the principles which we have enunciated.

Besides acquainting ourselves thus with the different phases of architectural evolution with the aid of a very restricted number of monuments we shall use the canons which we shall have already established in order to fix the date of all the others by their external aspect alone.

The archæologist who knows these canons can also find out the age of edifices in the same manner as the geologist distinguishes the age of sedimentary strata. He can know that such an edifice dates from the seventeenth century, depending only upon the *motifs* of ornamentation. It will be sufficient for him to observe the form of *kūḍus* or of the *bōdigais* just as the geologist, guided by the form of the fossils, affirms that such a rock is primary because it contains trilobites, that such a layer is secondary or tertiary according as it contains ammonites or cerithes.

In this little work, in which we attempt to show the evolution of Dravidian architecture, we shall study only the *motifs* of ornamentation, that is to say, that which is due to the chisel of the sculptor, and we shall pass on in silence all that which is related to the art of the engineer.

Such neglect will be incomprehensible in the study of the evolution of Gothic architecture.

The object of French architects of the Middle Ages was to construct vaults with materials of small size, and the history of Gothic architecture is the history of the investigation of the proper disposition of these materials, that is the solution of a question of mechanics.

The plan of edifices, the convergence of joints, the thrust of vaults were in the Gothic art primordial considerations.

This is not the case in the Dravidian art. The Hindus of Southern India had never any necessity for solving such questions. The great *vimānas* such as those of Tanjore, the great *gōpurams* like those of Trichinopoly and Madura, are only heaping up of stone in which the art of the engineer is almost nothing.

Nature permits the Hindu architect to construct immense halls or *manṭapams* by placing large slabs of granite upon monolithic pillars. The methods of construction are, therefore, very elementary; the details of the sculpture are very interesting, and the history of the architecture of Southern India reduces itself to the history of ornamentation.

This study will be entirely independent of æsthetic considerations. It is incontestable that there are in the Dravidian art very beautiful things, but the appreciation of beauty is often a question of taste, and we do not pretend to make any criticism of art. We think that architecture can be interesting whatever be the opinion which one has of the æsthetic sense of the Hindus. By systematic observation of the rules according to which the edifices have been constructed and by the employment of technical terms, we shall attempt to treat the subject in a purely scientific fashion.

CHAPTER II

CONTEMPORARY ARCHITECTURE

TEMPLES are still constructed in our own days, and although the modern workmen have before them European monuments, they are not inspired by the foreign *motifs* ; they build always following the architectural tradition which they have received from their ancestors.

Neither does one see in the pagodas constructed in recent times the triangular pediment of the Greeks, or the vaulted arch of the Romans, or the pointed arches of France. It will be illogical, in fact, to build in Southern India according to methods created on another soil and in a different climate. Why construct vaults with convergent joints when one can employ huge slabs of granite; why construct pointed roofs in a sunny country? The pagodas with their immense circuits which contain ponds and pillared-halls are perfectly adapted to the Hindu civilization, and it will be difficult to replace them by the edifices intended for other civilizations.

Just as animal species are subject to the law of 'Adaptation to the surroundings', architectural species adapt themselves to materials, to societies and to climates.

In order to study contemporary architecture, we must repair to temples in construction and speak to the workmen themselves, while they work in their stoneyard.

We have had before us the plans which they use, we have been able to sketch and photograph the stones at the moment when the chisel shapes them in the form of capitals or of corbels. Finally we have asked the sculptors, and they have given us written in Tamil, and orally, the names of every *motif*, of every moulding. That is the technical information which we shall try to recapitulate here.

This information we have obtained mostly while interrogating the workmen who constructed the pagoda of Tirupāpuliyūr (Cuddalore, New Town).

1. The Dravidian Order

One calls order, a horizontal division of architecture considered only with respect to decoration. In other words, when one considers monuments, which belong to the same order, one proves that they present the same superposition of basement, of pillar, of entablature, adorned in the same kind of moulding.

In Greek art, there exist three principal orders, called Doric, Ionian, and Corinthian which are well known.

In Dravidian art, there exists only one order, which we shall call the 'Dravidian order.'

Figure 17 (A) shows the name of every moulding.

It is necessary, however, to add some explanations.

1. The pedestal *upapīṭam* (உபபீடம்) is sometimes more simple, sometimes more ornamental than the type which we give here.

2. In the base *adiṣṭānam* (அதிஷ்டானம்) the moulding called *padmam* (பத்மம்) which is a sort of *doucine* represented by the petals of a lotus. It is not indispensable, because in certain parts of edifices, it is sometimes suppressed.

The moulding called *kumudam* (குமுதம்) is here a blunt corner [chamfered string-course (fillet)] but is sometimes a *tore*.

The moulding called *agrapaṭṭiyal* (அக்ரபட்டியல்) is a *listel*.

Very often it is found replaced by a *kabōdam* (கபோதம்) surmounted by a *yālam* (யாளம்). The two mouldings are identical to those which we shall describe further on, while speaking of the entablement *prastaram* (ப்ரஸ்தரம்).

3. The pilaster *stambham* (ஸ்தம்பம்) is sometimes square in section, and at other times octagonal. Often one sees a little ornament called *nāgabandham* (நாகபந்தம்).

Figure 1 represents the capital upon a very large scale. We give to this kind of capital the name of 'bulbous' capital on account of its bulbous form.

The *palagi* (பலகை) corresponds to abacus. It is supported by the petals of a lotus called *idal* (இதழ்)

Fig. 1. Bulbous capital.

Figure 2 represents with more technical details the corbel in the form of a flower which surmounts the capital and which is called *puṣpabōdigai* (புஷ்பபோதிகை).

4. The entablement consists of four members *uttiram* (உத்திரம்), *ērādakam* (ஏராதகம்), *kabōdam* (கபோதம்), and *yālam* (யாளம்).

The larmier *kabōdam* (கபோதம்) is always ornamented with the *kūḍu* (கூடு) [1]

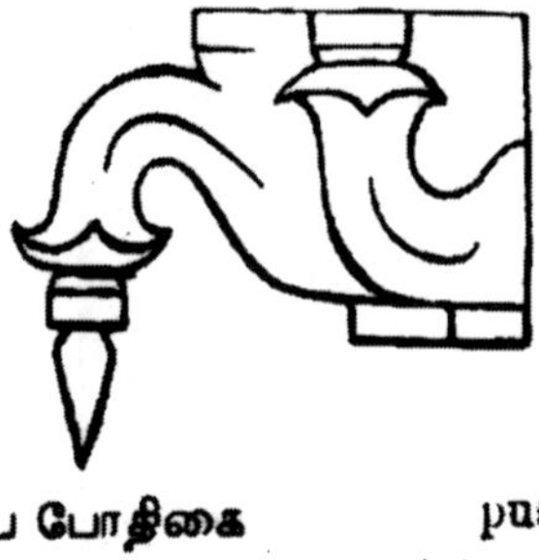

புஷ்ப போதிகை pushpabôdigai.

Fig. 2. Flowery Corbel.

[1] In regard of these conventional forms the following remarks of Lepsius would be useful. For even the 'heraldic style' has still its recognized place, and is a conventional but not an ignorant or barbarous conception such as any individual may at his pleasure repudiate. Even the real artist would not disdain this style in its proper place, but rather would impress it with his own mark which the real connoisseur would recognize.

Convention, if not always so comprehensible as in this case, was at all periods, as it is still, an important, nay an indispensable element in art.' (Bell's *Egyptian Architecture* quoted above, pp. 214 and 15). S.K.

Figure 3 represents two *kūḍu* one (B) ornamented, the other (A) simple. The central part is called *gandharvamukham* (கந்தர்வமுகம்) because there is often in that place the head of a *gandharva*. The central part is surrounded with foliage called *koḍi* (கொடி). The upper part is adorned with the head of a lion *simha-mukham* (சிம்மமுகம்).

Fig. 3. Cornice: (A) Kūḍu without Ornament. (B) Kūḍu with Ornament. (C) Yāḷam.

The moulding called *yāḷam* (*vide* Fig 4) is so called because it is decorated with lions with the trunk of an elephant called *yāli*. (யாளி).

5. The attic is formed of different kinds of little pavilions. The form of the pavilions differs according to their position upon the edifice. Those which are at the angles of the edifice (Fig. 4) are called *karṇakūḍu* (கர்ணகூடு); they have a roof of square or circular section and are surrounded by a single *urn, stūpi* (ஸ்தூபி). Those which are placed in the middle are called *śālai* (சாலை). They have an elongated roof and have three *stūpis*. Between the *karṇakūḍu* and the (*śālai*) are found some kinds of little windows called *panjaram* (பஞ்சரம்).

கர்ணகூடு Karṇakūḍu. பஞ்சரம் Panjaram. சாலை Śālai.

Fig. 4. Attic—[Note: the size of the Karṇakoḍu is double that of the Panjaram; but it is only of the size of the Śālai.

Figure 5 gives an idea of the disposition and the form of the pavilion of a modern temple.

In front of the pavilions are placed frequently statues of baked earth, representing personages, who are mostly gods.

Concerning the relative dimensions of the different parts of the edifice, it is of importance to note that, if one takes them as combined, the height of the *adishtānam* (அதிஷ்டானம்) is 2, the part called *stambham* (ஸ்தம்பம்) amounts to 1, and the part called *prastaram* (ப்ரஸ்தரம்) to a height equal to 1 (*vide* Fig. 1).

2. Ornamentation of Walls

Dravidian monuments are not generally made of windows. The walls cannot, however, remain bare. One employs two kinds of ornaments.

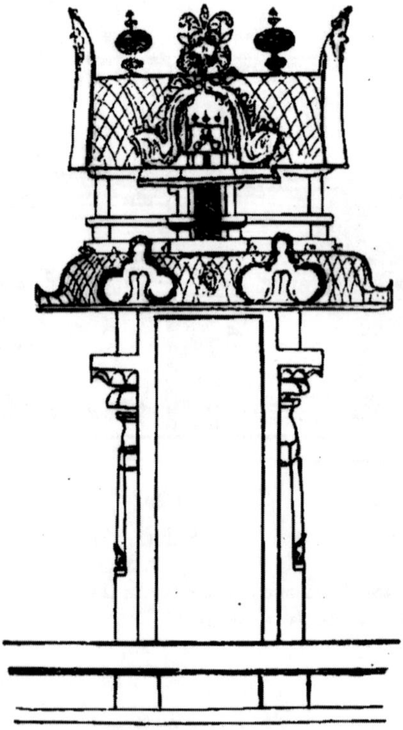

(*a*) The niche, *gōṣṭa-panjaram* (கோஷ்டபஞ்சரம்) is intended to contain images of divinities sculptured in high relief. Nevertheless they often remain empty.

கோஷ்டபஞ்சரம்
Fig. 6. Gōṣṭapanjaram

Fig. 5. Upper Part of a Modern temple (at Tiru-pāppuliyūr) showing the disposition of the pavilion.

Figure 6 shows the ornamentation of the frame of a niche. On either side of the niche are pilasters and above it a little pavilion, which, as the name indicates, ought to be a *panjaram*, but which is often (as in Fig. 6) a *śālai*.

The niches adorn generally the parts of walls which project in the front.

The parts of the edifice which are found in the background (in retreat) are adorned by the *kumbhapanjaram*.

(*b*) The *kumbhapanjaram* (கும்பபஞ்சரம்) is a pilaster the rôle of which is purely decorative (Fig. 7).

கும்பபஞ்சரம்
Fig. 7. Kumbhapanjaram.

As its name indicates, the pilaster is characterized by two *motifs*: in the lower part a sort of vase called *kumbham*, and the upper part a little pavilion (*panjaram*).

3. The Edifices

Figure 8 is the plan of a temple of Śiva in its essential dispositions.

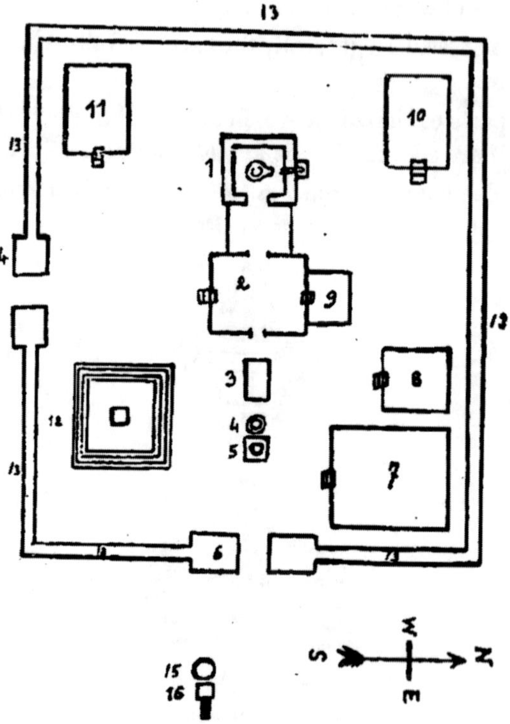

Fig. 8. Plan of a temple of Śiva

(1) Vimāna (விமானம்) in the centre at which is found the sanctuary Garbhagṛham (கர்ப்பக்கிருகம்) in the midle of which is found the Lingam (லிங்கம்)

(2) Mantapam (மண்டபம்) (3) Nandi (நந்தி)

(4) Dvajastambam (த்வஜஸ்தம்பம்) (5) Balipīṭam (பலிபீடம்)

(6) Eastern Gōpuram (கோபுரம்) (7) Kalyāṇa-manṭapam (கல்யாணமண்டபம்)

(8) Sanctuary of Naṭēśa (நடேசன்)

(9) Sanctuary of Pārvati (பார்வதி) (The sanctuary of Pārvati ought to be placed in front of the Gopuram at the South).

(10) Sanctuary of Subramaniar (சுப்பிரமணியர்)

(11) Sanctuary of Piḷḷāyār (பிள்ளையார்)

(12) Tank (kuḷam, குளம்)

(13) Sorrounding wall (madiḷ, மதில்)

(14) South Gōpuram

(15) Tēr (தேர்) (16) Ladder with steps to mount car

The buildings which constitute the pagoda *Ko-il* or ***Koyil*,** (கோயில்) are generally grouped without much order.

Nevertheless the pagoda ought to be oriented, that is to say, the gate of the sanctuary and in general all the gates which lead to the sanctuary ought to be turned to the east, in such a manner that it often happens that the sun, in rising on certain days in the year, throws its light on the *Lingam* which is in the sanctuary.

At the entrance to the temple are found one or more cars (in Tamil, *tēr* தேர்) which serve to carry the gods in the processions on festival days.

The lower part of the car is made of a special kind of wood of a tree of the family Bassia, called in Tamil *iluppai* (இலுப்பை.)

The monumental entrances of the temples are called *gōpurams* (கோபுரம்).

The principal is the one on the east; there ought to be a *gōpuram* also on the south; those on the north and the west are optional.

Figure 9 gives very simple examples of *gōpuram*.

Fig 9 Gōpuram.

The door *vāyil* or *vāśal* (வாயில் or வாசல்) is ordinarily twice as high as it is wide. The height is often considerable. The two shutters (flaps of a door) are made of wood and have partitions.

The number of stages *nilai* (நிலை) is always odd. Starting from nine stages, a *gōpuram* can be considered as being of the first greatness.

The stages are ornamented with little pavilions (*śālai*) சாலை and *karṇakūḍu* (கர்ணகூடு).

The *śālai* in the middle is prominent, much bigger than the others, and pierced with a window (the only one in the front). Before the pavilions, some statues of baked earth represent the divinities of worship which belong to the pagoda.

Among the statues, there are those which are obligatory: they are *dvārapālas* (த்வாரபாலர், door-keepers), on either side of the window. They are turned towards the window, to which they point. The one which is turned to the right side places the left foot upon a club placed on the right, and inversely.

It is to be remarked that the number and the disposition of the pavilions are the same at every floor (stage), only the dimensions vary.

When the *gōpurams* are new, they are painted completely and the statues, which adorn them, are painted in richer colours.

The surrounding walls, மதில் (*madil*) of which the *gōpurams* form the entrance are rectangular, surmounted with figures representing the bull (*Nandi*). It is a statue of Garuḍa when the temple is dedicated to Vishṇu.

When one enters by the *gōpuram* on the east of a temple of Śiva one finds successively before him the *balipīṭam* (the seat of sacrifice), the *dvajastambham* (த்வஜஸ்தம்பம்) and the Nandi (*vide* Fig. 10).

கோபுரம் பலிபீடம் த்வஜஸ்தம்பம் நந்தி லிங்கம்
Gōpuram Balipīṭam Dvajastambham Nandi Lingam

Fig. 10. Insignia in a temple with Siva. (The Lingam is seen in a side.)

Within the walls of temples are found sacred tanks *kuḷam* (குளம்) and *manṭapams* (மண்டபம்), resting places where the gods are every year carried on festival days (Fig. 11).

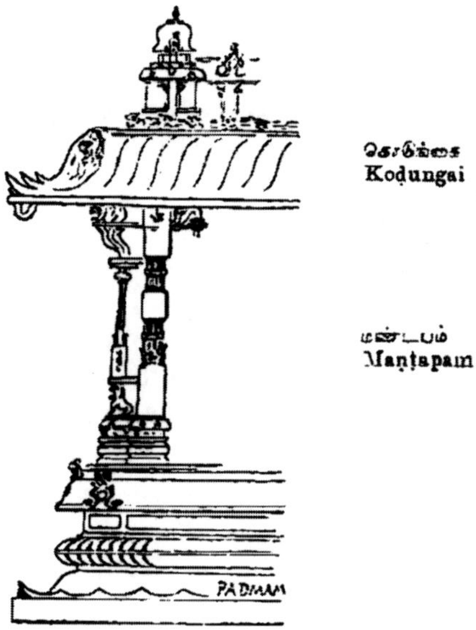

Fig. 11. Manṭapam—One will notice the Cornice with double curves which bears the name Koḍungai.

The *manṭapams* are not furnished with walls; the roofing is formed of large slabs of granite supported by monolithic pillars.

The base of the edifice is an *adiṣṭānam* identical with that which we have described formerly. One gets to the upper part of that base by a ladder, the balustrade of which is sculptured as indicated in figure 12.

சுருள்யாளி
Surul-yali

Fig. 12. Steps up to a Manṭapam.

The kind of pillar used principally in the *manṭapams* is the pillar with a cubical capital called *tūṇ* (தூண்).

Figure 13 which represents a little *manṭapam* at Tirupāpuliyūr shows the view of that kind of pillar. One will find the picture of a *tūṇ* with the technical terms explained in Figure 14.

Fig. 13. Maṇṭapam Tirupāpuliyūr.

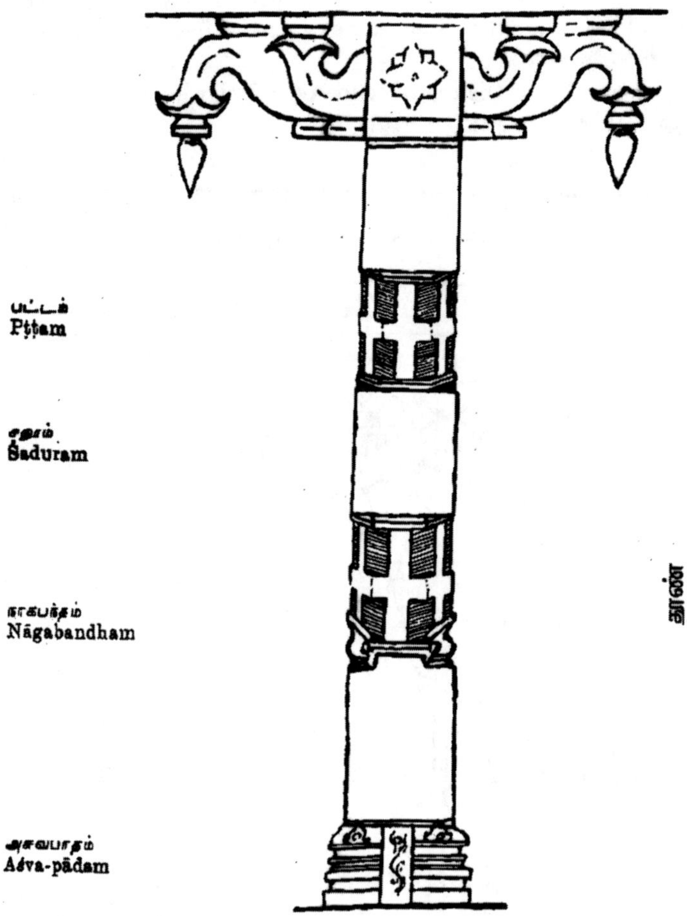

Fig. 14. Tūṇ (pillar with modern cubical capital).

The pillar is always raised by a base *aśvapādam*. It is formed of three cubical parts called *śaduram* (சதுரம்) and of two prismatic parts with facets called *paṭṭai* (பட்டை).

One sees often upon the *tūṇ*, as upon the pillar with the cubical capital, the little ornament called (*nāgabandham*; நாகபந்தம்) because its form recalls that of the hood of a cobra (*nāga*).

The pillar with the bulbous capital (Fig. 2) is rarely used alone to support the vaults of *manṭapams*; but a very frequent and even almost general case is that of the association of pillar with a bulbous capital, and that with a cubical capital in one and the same stone called (*aṇiveṭṭikkāl* அணிவெட்டிக்கால்).

Figure 15 is the reproduction of a design representing an *aṇiveṭṭikkāl* supporting a vault.

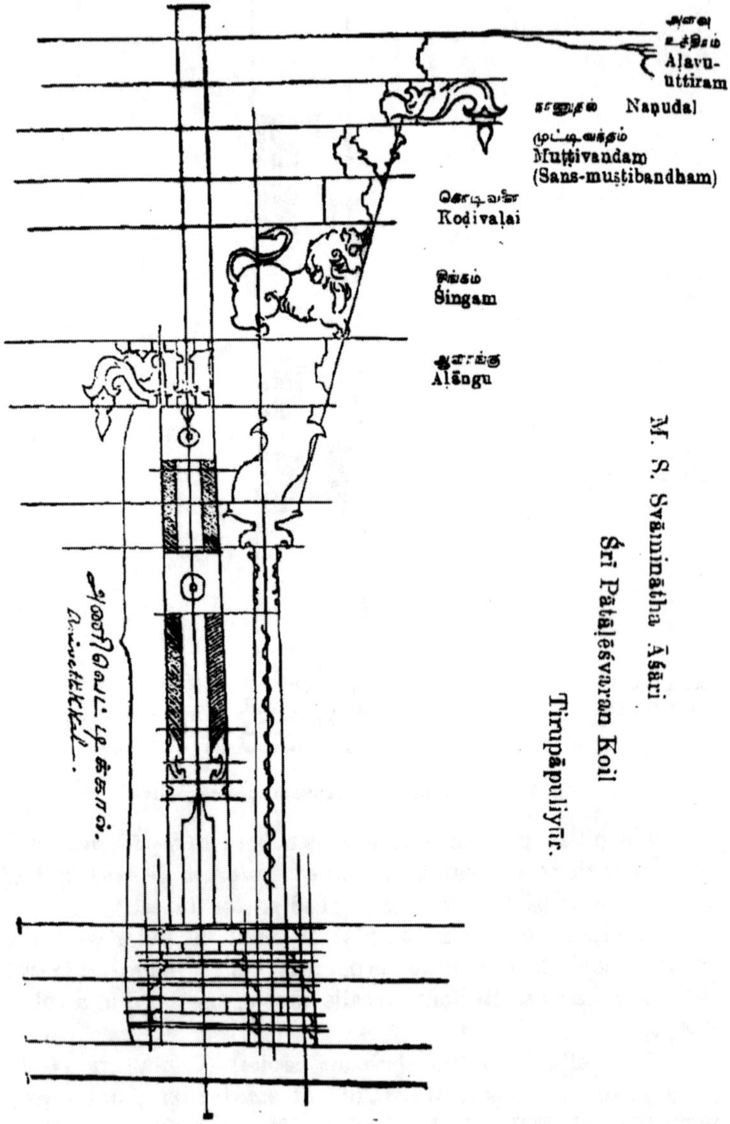

M. S. Svāminātha Āsāri
Śri Pātāḷeśvaran Koil
Tirupāpuliyūr.

This design, as the autographic address on one side indicates, has been made by the architect of the temple of Tirupāpuliyūr, M. S. Svāminātha Āśāri, Śrī Pāṭāḷēśvaran Koil, Tirupāpuliyūr.

Very often the pillar with the bulbous capital of the *aṇivettikkāl* is replaced by a rearing animal, a horse or a lion (*simha*) or a lion with the trunk of an elephant (*yāḷi*).

The sanctuary (*garbhagṛham*) occupies the middle of a temple surmounted by a tower aptly called *vimāna* (விமானம்).

விமானம்

Fig. 16. Vimāna.

The divinity is always placed in the middle of the *garbhagṛham* upon a pedestal called *avuḍaiyār* (ஆவுடையார்) which serves to receive the liquid matter with which the god is bathed, and to throw it out of the sanctum by means of a channel called *gōmukham* (கோமுகம்).

The *garbhagṛham* is often called *mūlasthānam*.

Let us add finally that the course which surrounds the sanctuary bears the name of *suttupprākāram* (சுற்றுப்பிராகாரம்).

CHAPTER III

PALLAVA ARCHITECTURE

In the preceding chapter we have reviewed the principal elements which constitute modern architecture, and we have understood what the technical terms used to designate them, are.

It is with the aid of this knowledge that we undertake in this chapter the study of Pallava architecture.

Now, in studying this architecture we shall make two statements which are of capital importance.

1. The Pallava monuments which are the most ancient known in the Tamil country can alone make us know the origin of Dravidian art; thus while examining the constitution of the elements of Pallava architecture, we shall observe the very important fact that the works in stone are the copy of works in wood; and that the primitive type with which the architects are inspired are no other than that of the worker in wood, made into beams and planks, which was utilized in Southern India at the beginning of our era, and which is represented by the bas-reliefs of the *stūpa* at Amarāvati.

The Pallava temple is derived from the primitive hut,[1] and the Dravidian art is then of purely indigenous origin.

2. If now we compare the Pallava architecture with modern architecture, one notices the fact, which is not less important, that the differences are of little importance; that these differences are in the details of secondary importance; but that the elements themselves remain the same; that there is not any *motif* of the modern art which one does not find, with but slight modification in the Pallava art.

[1] This is exactly the conclusion arrived at in regard to all Indian architecture by Mr. Havell (*vide* Chapter II, *Ancient and Medieval Architecture of India*, John Murray). In respect of some elements at any rate this is true of Egyptian architecture (see p. 38 and note). The *Architecture of Ancient Egypt* quoted already. S. K.

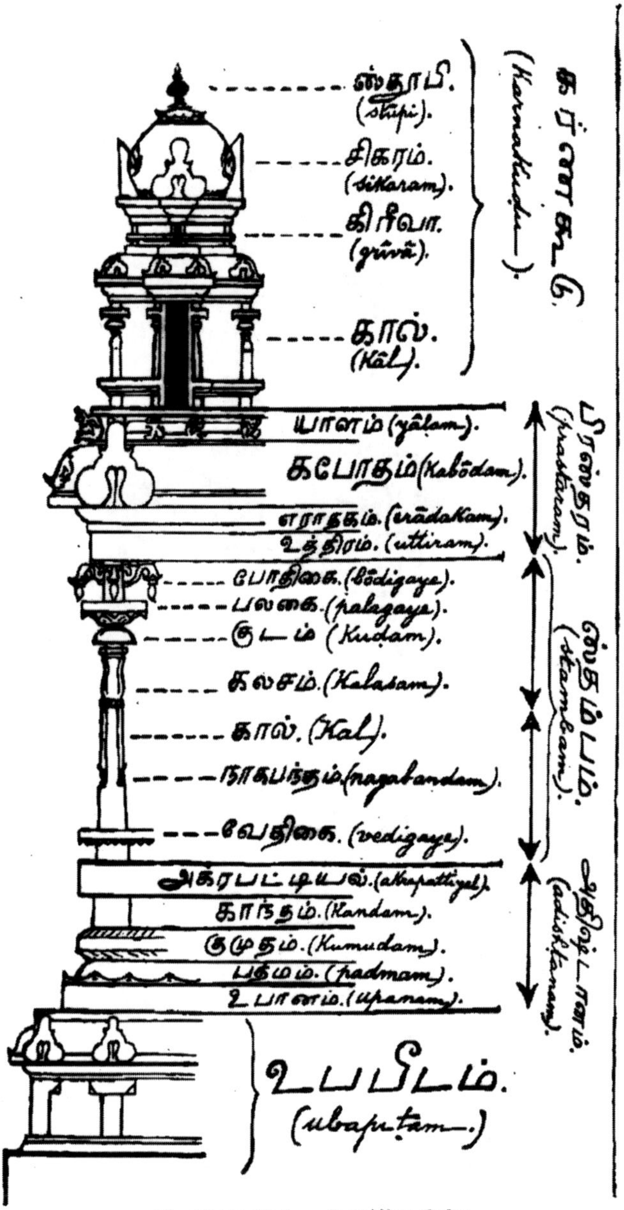

Fig 17 (A) Modern Dravidian Order

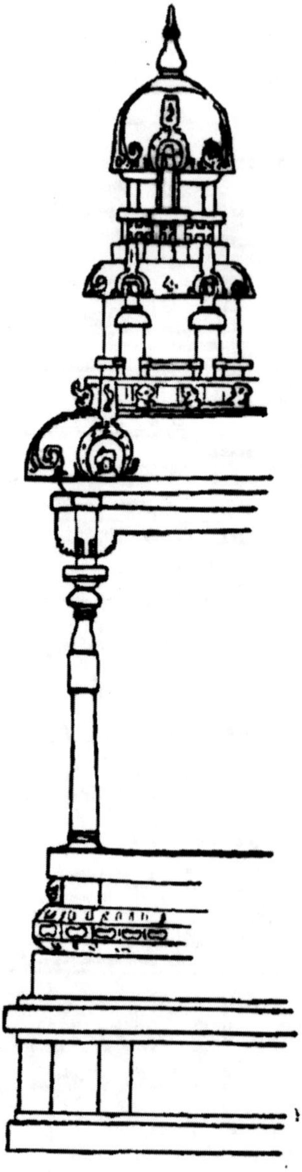

Fig. 17 (B) **Pallava**

From that time, when in the next chapter, we shall have shown that the modifications of details are produced progressively and slowly in the course of centuries, it will appear clearly that the Dravidian art, even as we have affirmed in Chapter I, is an art purely indigenous and that it has been transformed only by the path of natural evolution.

Pallava monuments are met with all over that part of the Tamil country which we have specially studied, which includes the three districts of North Arcot, Chingleput and South Arcot, and which formed that 'Toṇḍaimaṇḍalam' of which the capital Kāñchīpuram was that of the Pallavas.

Figure 17 (B) represents the Dravidian Pallava order.

It is necessary to remark that at first sight this order does not differ at all from the modern order which we have represented in Fig. 17 (A).

The two Figures 17 (A) and 17 (B) are, however, not identical, because if the order is the same in the two cases, the details of sculpture show differences.

In the first place then we may remark the following fact: to know the age of a Dravidian monument, it is essential to study with very great attention the details of ornamentation, because the main lines are the same.

Let us now compare every one of the parts of the figures 17 (A) and 17 (B).

The pedestal (*upapīṭam*) is wanting in very many of the Pallava monuments. It exists, however, in many of the others, e.g. in the base of the temple of Muktēśvara at Kāñchīpuram. (Plate XIX of *Pallava Architecture* by A. Rea.)

The base (*adiṣṭānam*) is almost identical in the figures 17 (A) and 17 (B).

We shall pass on next to the pilaster (*stambham*).

The shaft of a column (*kāl*) is almost identical with the modern shaft. The Pallava shaft is always without *nāgabandham*, an ornament which did not perhaps make its appearance till the twelfth century.

The Pallava bulbous capital is identical with the modern bulbous capital with the only difference that the moulding called *iḍal* is provided with indentations (notches). The notches of the *iḍal* made their appearance only in the twelfth century.

In many of the Pallava monuments the abacus (*palagai*) is purely and simply suppressed. In our days, on the contrary, the *palagai* exists always in the bulbous capital.

The corbel which is above the abacus differs entirely from the modern *bōdigai*.

The Pallava corbel is very simple: its profile is generally curved and it represents certainly the extremity of a joist.

In figure 18 one will see the simplest form of a Pallava corbel at Māmallapuram.

Very often, however, the corbel presents horizontal mouldings (figure 19). The *motif* is very probably borrowed from the art of the carpenter. The lines which follow seem to establish the fact:

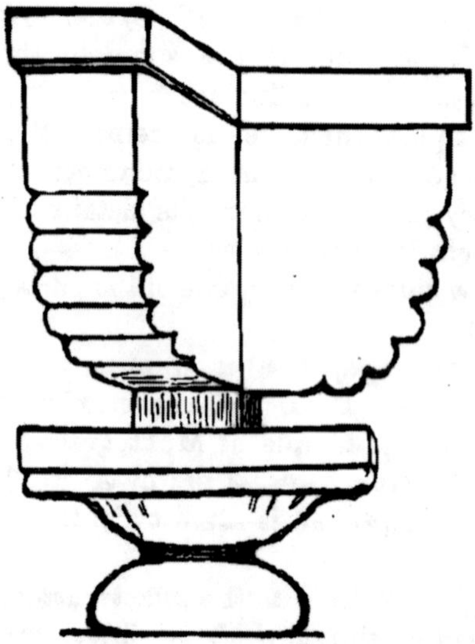

Fig. 19. Pallava corbel ornamented with mouldings in scrolls.

[Dictionnaire de l'architecture française du XIe au XVIe siècle, par Violet-le-Duc. IV. p. 309—corbel] '. . . The 'tradition of coverings in carpentry makes itself felt by the

Fig. 18. Interior of a cave at Mâmallapuram. One will notice the pillar and the corbel which supports the vault.

'presence of corbels which are placed under the tablettes '(tables) of cornices up to the end of the twelfth century.

'The church of Notre-Dame-du-Port, at Clermont, that 'of Saint Etienne of Nevers, possess cornices with corbels very 'interesting to observe. . . . It is evidently the imitation of an 'end of a *worked* joist. The cylinders which accompany the 'principal nerve are no other than the shavings produced by 'the hand of the carpenter to remove the nerve from the 'middle.

'It is sufficient to know how the workman can, with the 'chisel (*besaigne*) scoop out the end of a joist so as to reserve 'a supply, in order to know that the shavings, obtained with 'the work of the carpenter, reproduce the cylinders. The 'workman will remove from the two sides of the joist, with his 'sharp chisel, a series of chips so as not to split his wood; then 'he will cut them at their base, if he wishes to remove the 'renfort completely. Seeing that the *shavings* form an orna- 'ment one will have the idea at first of not cutting them at all, 'and the joists will have thus been placed. Later on, this 'decoration produced by the method of execution employed by 'the workman, will have been worked out in stone.'

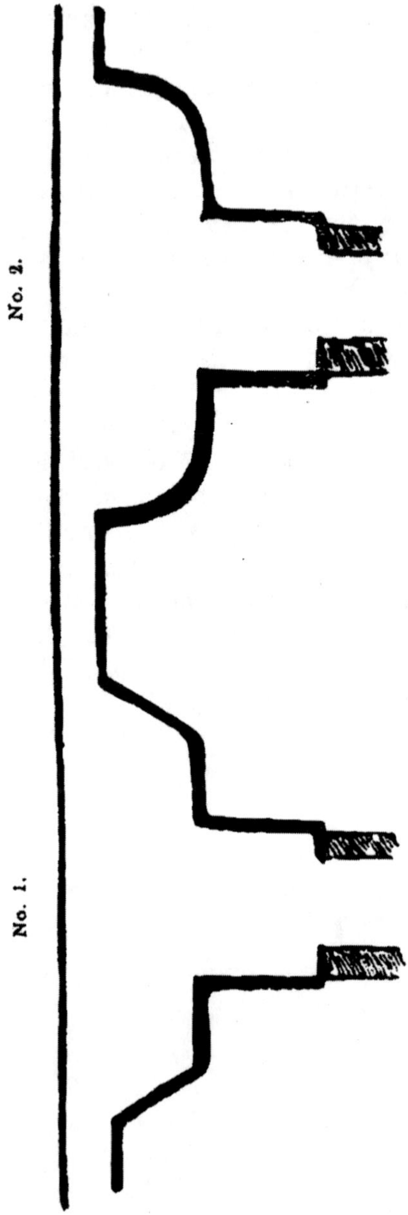

Fig. 20. Two forms of the Pallava corbel.

Very often the corbel does not have a curved profile but presents simply the appearance of the extremity of a joist which has been chamfered. (Fig. 20, No. 1.)

It is necessary, however, to remark that the circular form (No. 2 of Fig. 20) was peculiar to the Pallava epoch, while the other form (No. 1 of Fig. 20) would exist two or three centuries after the Pallava epoch.

The larmier (*kabōdam*) is ornamented, as in our days with *kūḍu* but sufficiently different from the modern *kūḍu*.

One should remember that the modern *kūḍu* is characterized by the head of a lion (*simha*), situated at the upper part and that from the mouth of the lion come out leaves.

The Pallava *kūḍu* [1] is characterized by the fact that there is no head of a lion on the upper part but that in that place there is an ornament of special form to which we give the name of 'the head of a shovel' on account of its likeness to a shovel.

The 'head of a shovel' is a distinct characteristic of the *kūḍu* of the Pallavas.

Figure 21 represents two kinds of *kūḍus* of the Pallava epoch.

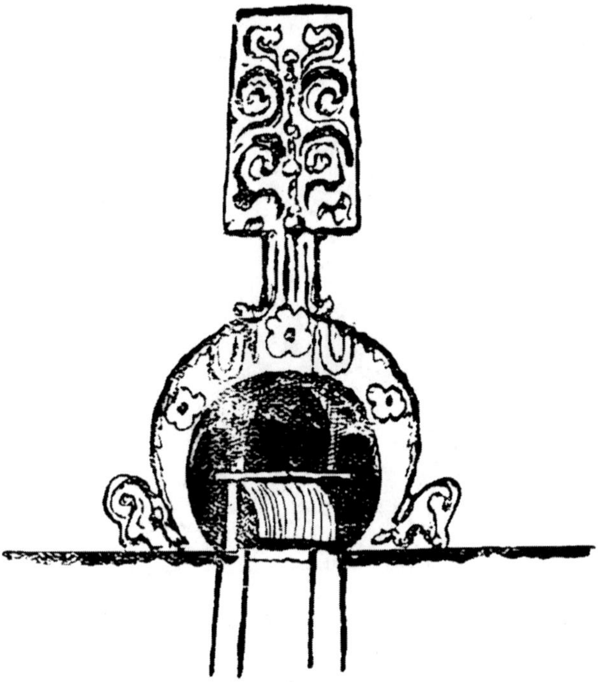

Fig. 21. Pallava Kūḍu with shade.

[1] The *kūḍu* seems reminiscent of a thatched roof. This roof has to be broken open in the places where the upright posts and the horizontal beams join. When cocoanut plaits are the material of roofing, these are bent over at the place letting in a little light and providing an opening for access of air. When the thatch gave place to other kinds of roofing this adjunct of necessity remained an ornament. S. K.

The form No. 1, Figure 21 shows that although the *kūḍu* is no other thing than a little gable end, *it* is a new proof of the fact that the Pallava architecture is derived from the art of the carpenter.

The *kūḍu* is no other than the extremity of a roof in the form of a *vault*. One meets with it frequently in the Buddhistic buildings and in particular those of the tope at Amarāvati (fig. 22).

The Pallava *kūḍu* of the kind No. 1, Figure 21 is characterized by the presence of a little roof placed in the centre and forming a sort of a little shed.

On the contrary the kind of *kūḍu* No. 2 is distinguished by the head of a *Gandharva* in its centre. The *kūḍu* being in fact a gable-end could serve as a skylight (a garret-window) and that is what justifies the presence of a human head which appears to look through the window.

Fig. 21. (No. 2) Pallava Kūḍu with the head of Gandharva.

The *Gandharva* has the characteristic aspect of the Pallava epoch, by its abundant hair and its two big ear-rings.

The part of the edifice called *kāl* which serves as a pedestal to the pavilion and which is indispensable in the modern art does not often exist in the Pallava art. The *rathas* of Māmallapuram do not always possess those.

It exists nevertheless in all the Pallava monuments of Kānchīpuram.

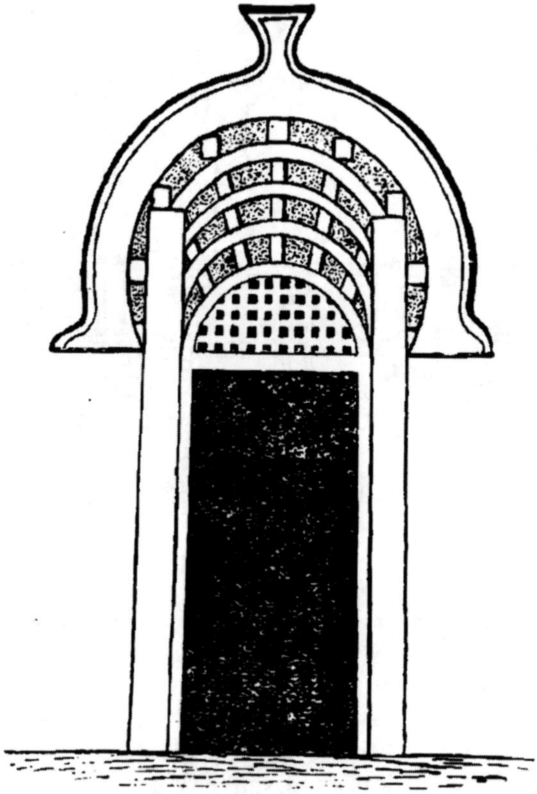

Fig. 22. The doorway of a Hindu monument of the Buddhist Age.

One will see by comparing Figure 17 (A) and Figure 17 (B) that the Pallava *kāl* differs from the modern *kāl* with regard to the detail that in the Pallava architecture the *kāl* has two windows while there is only one in modern architecture.

Figure 23, which represents two pavilions of Dharmarāja Ratha at Māmallapuram shows very well that in the beginning the pavilions were copies of little edifices of wood. One will specially notice that there exists a balustrade formed from beams of wood crossing one another which is very characteristic (cf. Figures 23 and 24.).

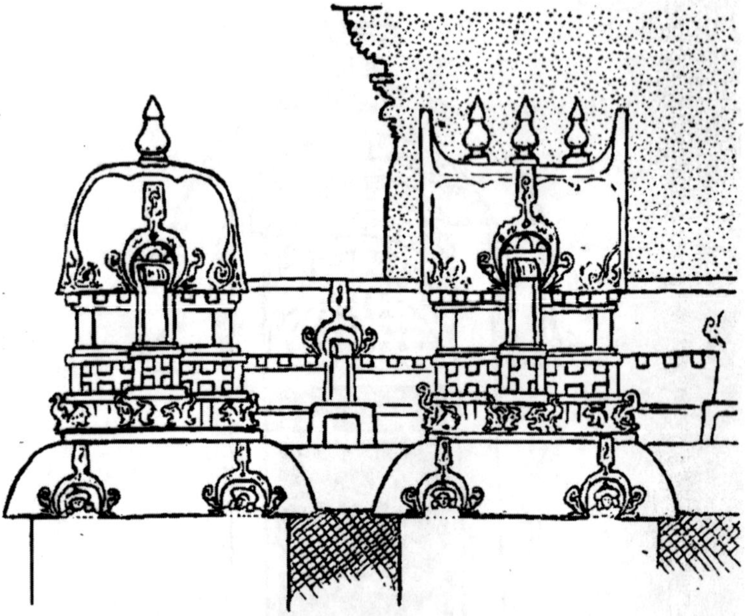

Fig. 23. Pavilions of the Dharmarājaratha at Māmallapuram.

The tops (*stūpis*) which decorate the crown-posts of roofs have very probably an origin which is explained by the construction in wood of the pavilions. The beams which support the vault being made of wood, run the risk of rotting on account of the influence of rain water. The upper extremities of the beams are covered with pots of baked earth which protect them. This is undoubtedly the origin of *stūpis*.[1]

It is necessary finally to speak of the pillar with a cubical capital which is found very often in Pallava caves.

[1] The inverted pot can be seen in all the more substantially erected sheds of the locality even now. In the case of conical roofs it is a single pot and in the case of long sheds there is a line of them, the number varying with the number of posts.—(S. K.)

Fig. 24. 'Arjuna Ratha' of Māmallapuram.

Figure 25 represents a pillar of the kind with more of details. It differs from a modern *tūn* represented in figure 14 in that essential detail that the Pallava *tūn* has its edges bent in the middle only. It has then two cubical parts and not three as in figure 14. The cubical parts are ornamented with the flowers of the lotus almost analogus to the flowers of lotus which adorn the rails of Buddhistic monuments.

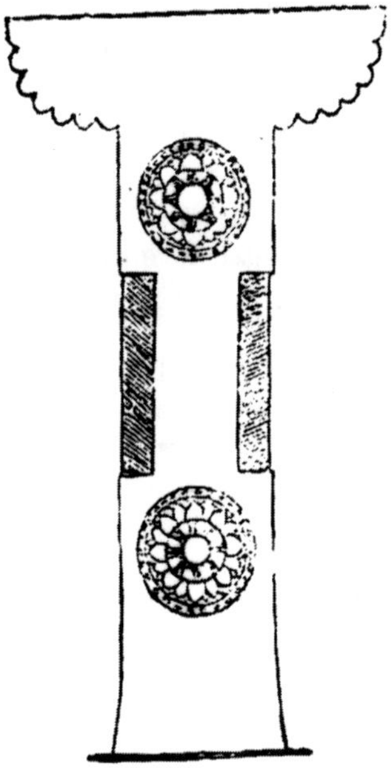

Fig. 25. Pillar with a cubical capital of the Pallava period.

The form of the pillar with the cubical capital of the Pallava epoch indicates clearly its origin. It is simply a square beam of which the sides have been bent in the middle of its height, reminding us thus of the appearance of the 'rails' in wood of the Buddhistic *stūpas*.

What we have said in this chapter is sufficient to show undoubtedly

1. that the Pallava architecture does not differ essentially from modern architecture and that the differences are only in details of ornamentation.

2. that the Pallava architecture is derived directly from the art of the carpenter and that the temples of the Pallavas are only the copy in stone of the house built of wood.

From the latter point we shall deduce the following inferences :—

1. If there do not exist in Southern India monuments prior to the seventh century, it is because the temples, monasteries, etc., ought to have been built in wood before that epoch.

2. From the very beginning Dravidian art is a purely indigenous art.

In the following chapter we shall try to show that the differences which exist between Pallava art and modern art are the result of a very slow evolution and that the *motifs* of ornamentation have been transformed only because the workmen have attempted to perfect their modes of decoration.[1]

[1] For more ample information regarding Pallava architecture, the reader is recommended to consult *Pallava Antiquities* by the same author, with thirty-two plates—published by Probsthain Co., 41, Great Russell Street, London, 1916.—(S. K.)

CHAPTER IV

THE EVOLUTION OF *MOTIFS*

We have said in the preceding chapters that there are very few essential differences between the most ancient and the most modern temples. The differences are those of details only. It is essential then to study carefully those of the details which have varied most in the course of centuries, and to trace the history of the *motifs* of ornamentation in order to characterize the different phases of the evolution of Dravidian architecture. The *motifs* of ornamentation are not all indeed equally evolved. In the same space of time, certain parts of an edifice have changed very much, while others have not changed in form. Thus then, in order to ascertain the age of a monument with certain approximation, it is necessary to examine particularly the *motifs*, which have evolved in a very characteristic manner. It is the study of these transformations which we shall enter on first.

In the second place it is essential to recall here that we are studying specially the monuments of the three districts of North Arcot, Chingleput and South Arcot. The study of the evolution of Dravidian architecture will thus be less general perhaps, but more precise. One understands indeed that the same *motifs* of ornamentation could, at a particular epoch, not have absolutely the same form in the north and in the south of the Tamil country. One can then formulate a law while studying a very limited region.

Finally, we do not pretend to study all the temples of the region in order to compare the architecture of every part of the edifice with the inscriptions engraved thereon. However restricted may be the region which we shall study, to study absolutely all the temples of that region will of necessity make very considerable work.

Here then is exactly the point in question.

In the course of numerous journeys which we have made in that part of the Tamil country which adjoins Pondicherry (districts of North Arcot, Chingleput and South Arcot), we believe we have noticed certain principles, certain general laws, which are always found to be verified.

These principles we are going to expound here, while proposing to consider them as demonstrated until they are proved to the contrary.

It is essential then to archæologists and to epigraphists of the Tamil country to verify the accuracy of what we have advanced.

Let us hope that the final verifications will only confirm what we have affirmed.

In order to follow pretty closely the evolution of the architecture, it is necessary to group century by century the monuments, the age of which is well known.

We cannot do this in such a small work as the present one; yet we shall divide the history of the architecture into a small number of periods. It appears to us that this history could be divided into five epochs, almost equal in duration, each lasting about 250 years.

This division is purely arbitrary, since art has changed by insensible evolution and not in a discontinuous manner. Nevertheless this division into five periods appears to us to be useful for the convenience of discussion. The five epochs are the following :—

1. Pallava epoch (A.D. 600 to 850).
2. Early Chōḷa epoch (A.D. 850 to 1100).
3. Later Chōḷa epoch (A.D. 1100 to 1350).
4. Vijayanagar epoch (A.D. 1350 to 1600).
5. Modern epoch (A.D. 1600 to the present time).

The names of the first four epochs are those of the royal dynasties which ruled successively in the Tamil country. These names of dynasties are found in most of the inscriptions engraved upon the temples and their choice for characterizing the styles is always indicated.

As examples of the monuments of the different epochs let us consider

1. for the Pallava epoch, the *rathas* and caves of Māmallapuram and the temples of Kailāsanātha and Vaikuṇṭha Perumāl at Kāñchīpuram ;

2. for early Chōḷa epoch, the temple which I discovered at Dādāpuram (South Arcot District, Tiṇḍivanam Taluk).

Fig. 26. Southern facade of the temple of Śiva at Dādāpuram (early chola style) the lower part of the photograph shews the inscription of Rājarāja which is engraved upon the same facade of the temple.

The temple, which bears an inscription of Rājarāja (figure 26) presents two peculiarities

(*a*) not having been restored in such a way that from the base to the summit, it presents all the distinct characteristics of a temple of the tenth century; (*b*) being well sculptured, it can be considered as a very honourable type of the style of 'Early Chōḷa'.

3. For the 'Later Chōḷa' period, 'the east *gopuram* at Chidambaram which dates from the king Kōpperuñjinga' who was a contemporary of the Chōḷa king Rājarāja III (G.O. Report for 1913-4, Part II, p. 82 and G.O. Report for 1905-6, Part II, paragraph 5.)

4. The monuments of the epoch of Vijayanagar are very numerous. They are, for example, the *gōpurams* of the pagoda of Villianūr (near Pondicherry).

5. Lastly for the contemporary period, we have already chosen the temple of Tirupāpuliyūr (Cuddalore New Town) which is not yet completed.

When there is a development by the path of evolution, one finds often that every period is characterized by the predominance of certain types.

In the preceding periods, certain forms exist only in the embryonic stage, then all of a sudden they undergo considerable development; after some time they become atrophied, and end sometimes by disappearing.

It is this which one can observe in the evolution of the Dravidian art. Let us consider, for example, the general form of buildings.

Rock-cut temples exist only in the Pallava period.

In the early Chōḷa period, it is the sanctuary of the temple, which one calls the *vimāna*, that assumes all of a sudden gigantic proportions, and it is this part of the edifice to which the architects give all their care. It is the epoch of grand *vimānas* of Tanjore and of Gangaikondapuram which rise up to 190 feet in height and which are magnificently ornamented. In the following epochs, the *vimāna* got atrophied, and was reduced to a pagoda, a few metres in height.

In the monuments prior to the later Chōḷa period, one finds only the embryo of the *gōpurams*. The temple of

Kailāsanātha at Kāñchīpuram has only a miniature *gōpuram*. Those of the temple of Tanjore (Early Chōḷa period) already a little more elevated, but it is at the later Chōḷa epoch that we find very grand and very beautiful *gōpurams* of Chidambaram and Jambukēśvaram.

At the epoch of Vijayanagar, they constructed still immense *gōpurams*, but it is easy to notice that this part of the edifice was not the most cared for; it is not upon these that the sculptor concentrated his efforts. At the Vijayanagar epoch, one sees a form of construction appear, which the former epochs did not know; it is the *manṭapam*, the resting place, where the gods are every year carried, which arrests the attention everywhere by its monolithic pillars, on which are sculptured horses, rearing lions and the gods everywhere. The *kalyāṇa manṭapam* of Hampi, of Conjeeveram, of Vellore, are characteristics of the art of the period.

The modern style is above all (especially) distinguished by its corridors. The most celebrated part of the temple of Madura is the *Pudumanṭapam*, which is only a vast corridor. But it is in the temple of Rāmēśvaram, that the predominance of corridors becomes manifest.

On the whole we can say that the Pallava period is that of sculptural rocks. The Early Chōḷa period that of grand *vimānas*, the Later Chōḷa period that of the most beautiful *gōpurams*. The Vijayanagar period is that of *manṭapams*. The modern period that of corridors.

The question of the history of the *motifs* of ornamentation arises in the following manner.

We have said that there are no essential differences between the styles of successive epochs of the history of architecture.

When an observer finds himself in the presence of a Dravidian monument, he will be greatly embarrassed in determining approximately the age of a monument. In fact, in order to distinguish the degree of antiquity of a Dravidian edifice it is necessary almost always to consider almost all the details of architecture.

It is essential then to determine certain rules necessary for, at least useful in, their appreciation.

1. The Corbel

Of all the parts of the edifice, that part, the form of which has varied in the most characteristic fashion is perhaps 'the corbel' which is placed below the capital of the pillars and of which we have already spoken.

Figure 27 shows the form of the corbel at different epochs. Nevertheless it is necessary to make a number of observations on the subject.

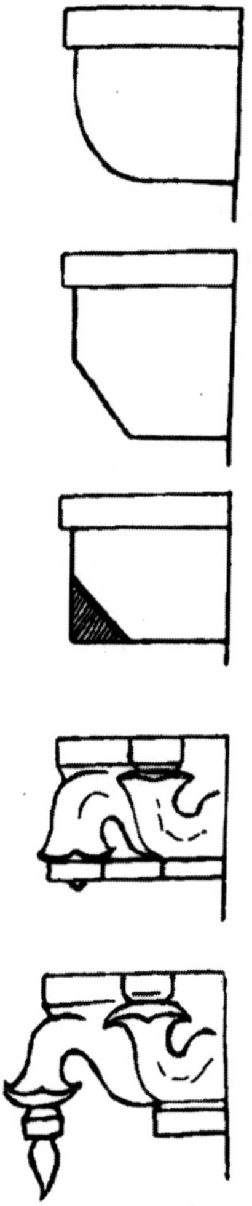

(1) Pallava A.D. 600 to 850

(2) Early Chola A.D. 850 to 1100

(3) Later Chola A.D. 1100 to 1350

(4) Vijayanagar A.D. 1350 to 1600

(5) Modern

Fig. 27. Corbels characteristic of the different periods

The corbel with a curved profile (1) Figure 27 sometimes simple, sometimes ornamented with 'rollers' of which we have spoken in the preceding chapter is exclusively Pallava. Nevertheless it is not the only one employed since frequently enough one finds the form (2) in the Pallava monuments.

It is still essential to say that this form is the most generally used at the Pallava epoch.

Never, in any Pallava monument, does one see the forms (3), (4) and (5).

For example never does one see the *pushpabōdigai* in the ancient temples; we affirm likewise that if one had just discovered a *pushpabōdigai* which can be attributed in a certain manner to the Pallava epoch, we shall abandon immediately all idea of evolution of the Dravidian art; the *pushpabōdigai* is essentially an ornament of the recent epoch.

The form (2) which is met with sometimes in the Pallava epoch is very general in the 'Early Chōḷa' epoch; but it disappeared completely in the other epochs.

The form (3) which appeared only at the end of the 'Early Chōḷa' and which is almost general at the 'Later Chōḷa' epoch did not disappear in the following epochs. It is met with still frequently at the epoch of Vijayanagar. But it is not the form (3) alone which was in use in the 'Later Chōḷa' epoch. In many of the monuments the corbel is fashioned in the form of *doucines* and little by little the form (3) becomes transformed into the form (4) which is that of (the flowers) of lotus falling down (drooping).

At the end of the 'Later Chōḷa' epoch, the monuments present often a peculiarity; the corbels which have already been completed, and taken the form (4), appear during the same like the corbels of the form (3).

The form (4) is distinguished from form (5) by the fact that, in the form (5), the flower of the lotus (*pushpa*) is completely detached from the rest of the stone and is terminated by a sort of finial (*pūmunai*). Let us not think that the form (5) existed before the sixteenth century.

The history of the 'Dravidian corbel' (figures 28 and 29) illustrates very well the meaning of the expression, evolution of the Dravidian art.

Pallava Early chola Later chola Vijayanagar Modern

Fig. 28. Evolution of the Corbel (view of three quarters)

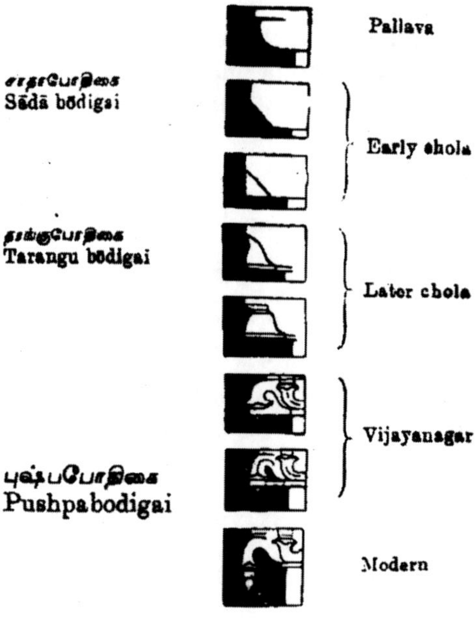

Fig. 29. History of the bōdigai

The ancient forms are derived from the art of the carpenter; the corbel is no other than the extremity of beams cut with the blows of the hatchet.

The modern forms of *bōdigai* are explained by the care which the sculptor has bestowed upon the stone to embellish that part of the edifice.

By what has preceded one sees that 'the Dravidian corbel' has often the same form at different epochs; that does not suffice the . to indicate the age of an edifice.

2. 'Idaḷ' and 'Nāgabandham'

We have said that the part of the capital which supports the abacus (*palagai*) is called *idaḷ*.

The *idaḷ* has the form of the calyx of a flower of lotus. Thus in Pallava and Early Chōḷa epochs, the petals of the flower were not represented. On the contrary in the later Chōḷa, Vijayanagar and Madura epochs, the extremity of the petals were represented in such a manner that below the abacus it appears to have a series of indentations (figure 30). The indentations go by the name of *munai* (முனை) in Tamil.

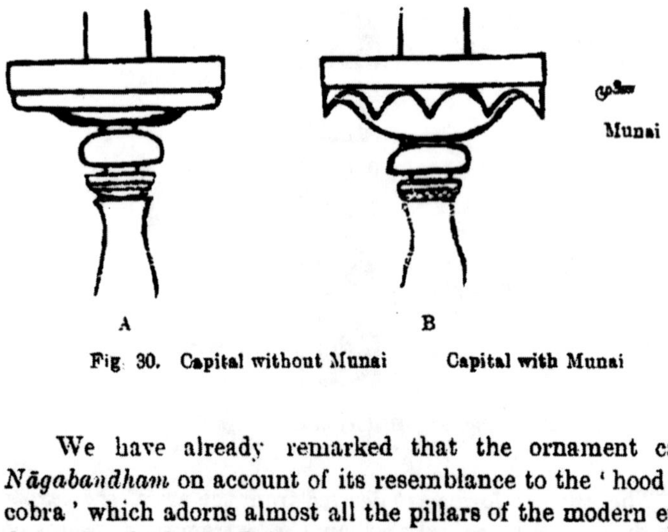

Fig. 30. Capital without Munai Capital with Munai

We have already remarked that the ornament called *Nāgabandham* on account of its resemblance to the 'hood of a cobra' which adorns almost all the pillars of the modern epoch does not exist in the Pallava epoch.

It made its appearance in the same epoch as the indentations of the *idaḷ*, i.e. to say at the end of the 'Later Chōḷa' epoch.

One can then say that every pillar on which one sees an *idaḷ* indented and *nāgabandham* is posterior to the twelth century.

Figure 31 shows the evolution of the pillar with bulbous capital where one can see the history of the three types which we have studied till now; the corbel, the *idaḷ* and the *nāgabandham*.

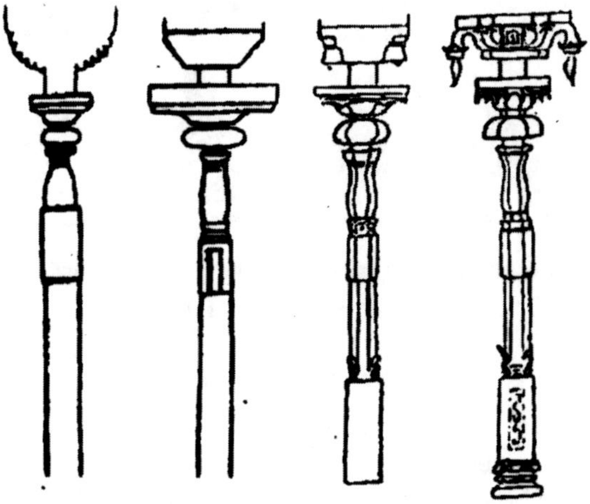

600 A.D. 1000 A.D. 1350 A.D. 1650 A.D.

Fig. 31. Evolution of the pillar with bulbous Capital

3. The 'Kūḍu'

We have already said that the Pallava *kūḍu* was characterized by the 'head of the shovel'. At other epochs the upper part of the *kūḍu* is always adorned with the head of a lion (*siṁha-mukham*). However, the leaves which adorn the circular part of the *kūḍu* differ in appearance at every epoch, in such a manner that it is often easy to know the age of an edifice by the appearance of the *kūḍu* itself.

Figure 32 shows the successive *aspects* of the *kūḍu* at the different epochs in the history of South Indian architecture.

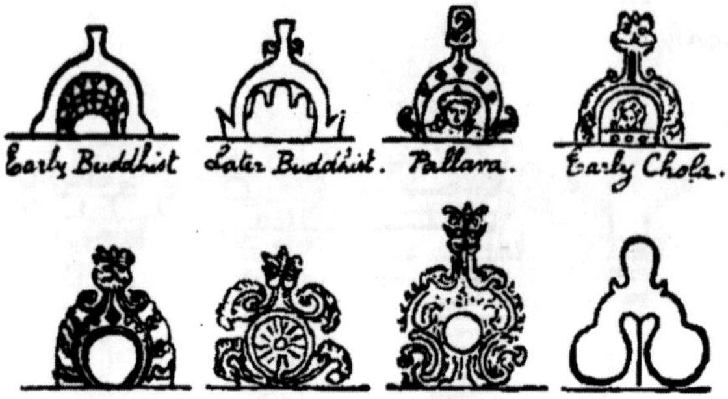

Later chola Paṇḍya Vijayanagar Modern

Fig. 32. Evolution of the Kūḍu

4. THE NICHE ('GŌSHṬA ')

The framing of niches where the images are placed differ according to their epochs.

Figure 33 (*a*) above shows the upper part of a niche of one of the *rathas* of Māmallapuram.

Fig. 33 (*a*). A. Pallava

The Figure 33 (*b*) shows the ornamentation of a niche of the 'Early Chōḷa.'

Fig. 33 (*b*). Early Chola

Figure 33 *(c)* shows a niche of the east *gōpuram* at Chidambaram, which can represent the style of the 'Later Chōḷa' epoch.

Fig. 33 (*c*). Later chola

Fig. 33. Evolution of the Niche

This kind of ornamentation is perhaps generally used still in our days. It is distinguished from the other two by the presence of *śālai*. We are able even to lay down the following principle: There does not exist any niche decorated with a *śālai* figure 33 (*c*) in the monuments prior to the eleventh century.

This characteristic allows us to affirm that a monument of which the niches are surmounted by a *śālai* is posterior to the eleventh century.

5. Kumbhapanjaram

We have already spoken of the ornament in studying modern architecture.

We have represented it in Figure 7.

The *motif* does not exist at all in the Pallava epoch.

In order to ascertain the origin of the *motif* it is necessary to examine attentively figure 26 which represents the temple of 'Śiva at Dādāpuram.'

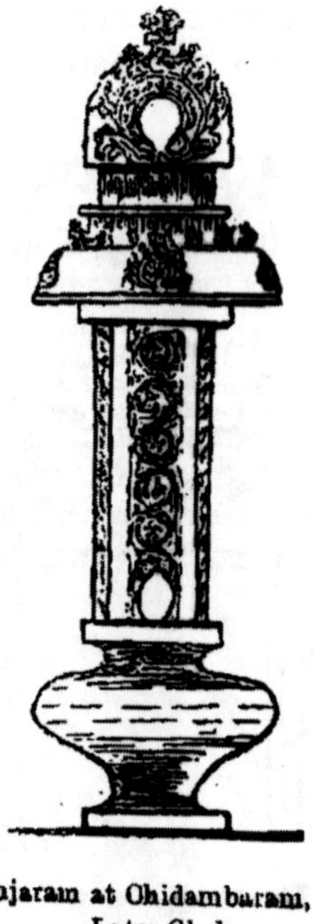

Fig. 34. Kumbhapanjaram at Chidambaram, XIIIth century, Period Later Chola

One does not see a *kumbhapanjaram* but a kind of niche which occupies its place, the general appearance of which is almost the same.

Figure 34. Later on (figure 34) the *kumbhapanjaram* appears, but of a manner different from the modern form.

6. The Pavilion

The appearance of the pavilion allows us less to characterize the age of edifices. Besides this part is very often restored, so that the upper part of the monuments is not always of the same style as its base. We have nevertheless attempted to show in figure 35 the appearance of pavilions in three different epochs.

Pallava — Later Chola — Vijayanagar

Fig. 35. Evolution of the pavilion

We hope that we have made it clear, in the small space we allowed ourselves, that Dravidian Architecture is of indigenous origin and has advanced by a course of evolution; that the structural development is little if anything at all, while the development has all along been one of ornamentation. The motifs that are essential to the study of this evolution have been described in this last chapter. It is to be hoped that the details given are adequate to illustrate our position, and will evoke the interest that the book is intended to awaken.